THIS JOURNAL BELONGS TO:

Made in the USA
Middletown, DE
09 February 2020

84455885R00113